ALASKA
Portrait of a State

ALASKA
Portrait of a State

GRAPHIC ARTS™ BOOKS

Library of Congress Control Number: 2005936448
International Standard Book Number: 978-1-55868-952-7

Captions and book compilation © MMVI by
Graphic Arts™ Books,
An imprint of Graphic Arts Books
P.O. Box 56118
Portland, OR 97238-6118
(503) 254-5591

Dust Jacket Design: Vicki Knapton
Interior Design: Jean Andrews

Fourth Printing
Printed in China

FRONT COVER: ◗ Hiking trails lead from Cottonwood Lake to Goat Mountain of the Chugach Range.
BACK COVER: ◗ The Eagle River Valley is a great place for snowshoeing—but beware! It is also natural habitat for moose, black bear, brown bear, and other wild creatures.
◀◀ Some scientists say the aurora borealis cannot be heard, but some observers disagree.
◀ Silver Horn, of Lake Beverley in Wood-Tikchik State Park, is one of two fjords in the area; the other one is the Golden Horn. Wood-Tikchik is the largest state park in America.
▶ Hoarfrost covers balsam poplars near Sheep Mountain, southwest of Tahneta Pass.

◄ The Killer Whale Clan dances at the Four Clans longhouse.
▲ This model Native Clan House at Totem Bight State Historical Park,
Ketchikan, incorporates both Tlingit and Haida art and architecture,
and could have housed thirty to fifty people.

▲ A mother Canada goose *(Branta canadensis)*
goes for a stroll in a quiet Alaska waterway, her goslings
swimming along behind. Canada geese generally migrate
south for the winter, then return to their northern
habitats for breeding in the spring.

▲ Near Anchor Point, the setting
sun silhouettes 10,016-foot Iliamna Volcano.
Glaciers cover most of the volcano. Iliamna regularly
vents steam yet it has been the least active
of the four Cook Inlet volcanoes.

▲ Tee Harbor, in the Juneau area of Southeast
Alaska, is home to crabbers—and their colorful pots and nets.
▶ Fishing boats are moored in Sitka Harbor, on Baranof Island. Sitka
is not only a busy industrial fishing harbor, it is also one of Alaska's
most popular ports for salmon and halibut fishing vacations.

▲ Near Sutton, frost outlines the
twisted limbs of a birch tree above Moose Creek.
► Mount Susitna, known by locals as the "Sleeping Lady," rises
across Cook Inlet from Earthquake Park, Anchorage.

◄ Rafting is a popular sport along the Copper
River. The three-hundred-mile-long river drains much of
the Wrangell and Chugach Mountains, emptying into the Gulf of Alaska.
▲ The Last Chance Mining Museum is located in the historic compressor building
of the Alaska Juneau Gold Mining Company, which operated in Juneau
from 1912 to 1944. The museum contains exhibits of industrial
artifacts associated with hard rock gold mining.

▲ Climbers en route to the summit of North
America's highest mountain, Mount McKinley, or Denali,
have reached the 19,000-foot level. They still have more than
1,000 feet to climb to reach the 20,320-foot summit.

▲ A paddler takes a break to hike along the aufeis ice piled
up alongside the Hulahula River in the Arctic National Wildlife Refuge.
Aufeis occurs when a river freezes over and the flowing water beneath is put
under increasing pressure. Eventually it finds a weak spot and breaks
through to the surface, only to freeze in layer after layer of aufeis.

▲ In Denali National Park, a bull moose ranges in search of a female. Though one should be wary of moose at any time of year, they are especially dangerous in fall, during the rut or mating season.

▶ A beaver in Denali works to place a willow branch in just the right position on the dam he is building.

◄ A pair of bald eagles *(Haliaeetus*
leucocephalus) perches on a branch in the Chilkat Valley.
▲ Females lay a clutch of one to three eggs, but usually two.
The eaglets generally hatch over a two- to three-day period.
Because of their size, older hatchlings dominate the
younger ones for food. In a three-egg brood,
the third chick has little chance of survival.

◄ A lynx seems ghostlike against the snow in the foothills
of the Takshanuk Mountains, in northern Southeast Alaska.
▲ An aerial view over the Kahiltna Glacier, on Mount McKinley,
shows rock and soil deposits, called moraine, mixed
with the ice flowing down the glacier.

▲ Fed from an ice field high above Juneau, Mendenhall Glacier
grinds and scours everything in its path as it carves its way down to
the sea. Dwarf fireweed *(Epilobium latifolium)* forms a colorful carpet in
the area around the Mendenhall Glacier, in Tongass National Forest.
▶ Nootka lupine *(Lupinus nootkatensis)* brightens St. Paul
Island in the Pribilof Islands.

◄ Mudflats along parts of the Lynn Canal provide habitat
for numerous bird species. At up to two thousand feet deep,
the ninety-mile-long canal is the deepest fjord in North America.
▲ The Chugach Mountains rise beyond Palmer Hay Flats
State Game Refuge. The Knik Arm of Cook Inlet
flows through the refuge.

▲ In Denali National Park, fading
blueberry bushes still add color in mid-September.
▶ Sitka is considered by many to be Alaska's
most beautiful seaside town.

◄ CLOCKWISE FROM TOP LEFT: Some 445 bird species have been sighted, including
● A great horned owlet *(Bubo virginianus),* keeping close watch on everything around;
● A willow ptarmigan *(Lagopus lagopus),* its plumage changing from summer to winter;
● Trumpeter swans *(Cygnus buccinator),* North America's largest native waterfowl; and
● A common loon *(Gavia immer),* its head thrown back to call in Wonder Lake.
▲ Homes are built on stilts along Hammer Slough on Mitkof Island, Petersburg.
The island is home to healthy wolf, black bear, deer, and moose populations.

▲ The Trans-Alaska Pipeline begins at Prudhoe
Bay on Alaska's North Slope and extends for eight
hundred miles over, under, and through the Brooks Range—
sometimes intersecting with the Dalton Highway—before reaching
Valdez, the northernmost ice-free port in North America. The
pipeline accounts for 25 percent of U.S. oil production.

▲ Once an essential part of Alaska transportion,
dog mushing is now enjoyed mainly as a sport. In 1972, it
was adopted as the official state sport. The 1,049-mile Iditarod
Trail Sled Dog Race is the most famous yearly event
that keeps mushing in people's minds.

▲ Dwarf birch *(Betula nana)* and willow line
a bluff above Upper Twin Lake, near the mouth of
Hope Creek, in Lake Clark National Park and Preserve.
There are more than thirty varieties of willow in Alaska.
▶ Myriad plants, including grasses, mosses, and a variety of tiny
flowers, provide a carpet of life in the tundra of Denali National Park.
Arctic tundra is a treeless area except for a few small shrubs.

◄ The setting sun paints sky and sea in pinks,
purples, and yellows at Coffman Cove in the Inside Passage.
▲ In June, a willow prepares to bloom in the Arctic National Wildlife Refuge.
Because permafrost in the Arctic inhibits root growth, plant life hugs
the ground. Willow trees that grow only six inches in height still
produce flowers, and the process of re-creation continues.

▲ CLOCKWISE FROM TOP LEFT: Caribou *(Rangifer tarandus)* roam Alaska's arctic and mountain tundra and northern forests. Examples of caribou in their varied habitats are:
◗ A bull caribou losing velvet, which supplies blood flow to its antlers. The red color will fade;
◗ Caribou heading south in August. They will return to their northern calving grounds in spring; and
◗ Female caribou and a days-old calf running across the tundra of Arctic National Wildlife Refuge.
▶ The arctic ground squirrel *(Spermophilus parryii)* is the only mammal that can lower its body temperature to below freezing, which helps it survive through the long arctic winter.

◄ In the rain forest of Chichagof Island, sulphur
shelf fungus *(Polyporus sulphureus)* grows on a tree.
▲ Fireweed *(Epilobium angustifolium)*—here mixed with wild
barley *(Hordeum vulgare ssp. spontaneum)*—is usually found
in wooded areas that have been cleared or burned off.

▲ Gislason Farm is a working dairy farm nestled in the
shadow of the Chugach Mounains in the Matanuska Valley. In 1935, as
part of the recovery from the Great Depression, an experiment was tried:
populate the Matanuska Valley with farmers. It was not a roaring
success, but it did give Alaska a new profile, as a farming state.
▶ A red auora lights the sky at Colorado Lake, Broad Pass.

▲ Patsy Ann was a bull terrior who stole the
hearts of Alaskans in the 1930s. Deaf from birth, she
somehow knew when ships were coming and rushed to the
docks to greet them, earning the label "Official Greeter of Juneau."
▶ An early morning view of Juneau's South Franklin Street
shows empty streets that will fill with thousands of
tourists arriving each day on cruise ships.

◄ Shooting star *(Dodecatheon jeffreyi)*
brightens the Palmer Hay Flats State Game Refuge.
▲ A grizzly or brown bear *(Ursus arctos)* fishes at
Brooks Falls, in Katmai National Park.

▲ Bearberry leaves add brilliant color in fall as
they turn from green to orange or red at Denali National
Park and Preserve. Bearberry is native to North America, ranging
from the Atlantic to the Pacific, and from California to Alaska.
▶ Upper Twin Lake is situated in Lake Clark National Park
and Preserve. Most of the preserve is designated
wilderness and is little used by people.

◀ The Lake Hood Air Harbor in Anchorage is the busiest
floatplane base in the world. The "flyingest" state in the nation, Alaska
boasts about six times as many pilots per capita as the rest of the United States.
▲ An icy Cook Inlet holds a reflection of the skyline of Anchorage. The bluffs
above the inlet, once an affluent neighborhood, became little
more than a pile of rubble in the earthquake of 1964.
The area is now preserved as Earthquake Park.

◄ Three-Hole Rock frames snow-covered mountains in Kenai Fjords National Park. The fjords are formed by a range of coastal mountains that are slowly sinking into the ocean, transforming its former glacial valleys into long fjords with steep, rocky walls.

▲ Moss campion *(Silene acaulis),* here shown in Chugach State Park in the Eklutna Glacier Valley, thrives in alpine regions.

▲ Alaska offers the ultimate in sport
fishing as well as commercial fishing ventures.
▶ When people think of sports activities in Alaska, they
usually think of fishing, hiking, mountain climbing, or
dog mushing—but golf has become a growing sport
in various parts of Alaska in recent years.

◄ A Sitka black-tailed deer *(Odocoileus hemionus)*
seems alert but calm on Mitkof Island near Petersburg.
▲ In Katmai National Park, a grizzly or brown bear *(Ursus arctos)*
has apparently had a hard day of fishing. He has simply
decided to take a nap on the sand.

▲ Independence Mine, an abandoned gold mine near
Hatcher Pass, is now part of Independence Mine State Historical Park.
Gold was found in the area in 1886, and in 1906, Robert Lee Hatcher began the
first lode mining operation in the area. The mine was permanently closed in 1951.
▶ More than 150 rustic cabins dot remote areas in the Tongass National Forest.
▶▶ The setting sun silhouettes the Fairweather Mountains near Point Adolphus.

◄ A Steller's jay *(Cyanocitta stelleri)*
in Kenai Fjords National Park searches for
food. The bird likes a wide variety, including small
vertebrates and arthropods, seeds, berries, and nuts.
▲ A commercial fishing trawler is hard at work in
Frederick Arm, in Alaska's Inside Passage.

63

▲ Pioneer Peak, reaching 6,398 feet above
sea level, rises beyond the Knik River Valley.
▶ A hiker uses a Tyrolean traverse to cross the lower
river at Keystone Canyon near Valdez.

◄ The Log Cabin Visitor Information Center
in downtown Anchorage is an attraction in its own right.
▲ No visit to Juneau would be complete without a stopover at
the Red Dog Saloon, where hordes of gold seekers gathered
to drink and carouse during the great Gold Rush of 1898.

▲ The Alaska Range is clearly dominated by Denali, and
Wonder Lake doubles the impact as it holds the reflection of the
mountain and the range in its depths. The Alaska Range extends
for about four hundred miles in South Central Alaska before
continuing southwest as the Aleutian Range.

◄ A sea kayak is beached at a rocky shore on an
island in Northwestern Fjord in Kenai Fjords National Park.
▲ An aerial view of Wood-Tikchik State Park shows a meandering,
braided river delta. A wilderness area covering more acreage than the
entire state of Washington, Wood-Tikchik is the nation's largest state park
and is home to moose, grizzly bears, eagles, salmon, and rainbow trout,
to name just a few of the animals that inhabit the area.

▲ A hoary marmot *(Marmota caligata)* checks out
Exit Glacier, in Kenai Fjords National Park. The body of
an adult marmot may reach as much as twenty-two inches long.
▶ A meadow in Eklutna Flats is carpeted with irises *(Iris setosa)*.
Eklutna Flats is a tidally influenced area situated at the
confluence of the Knik and Matanuska Rivers.

◄ Humpback whales *(Megaptera novaeangliae)*
spout at Point Adolphus, near Glacier Bay National Park.
▲ Clockwise from top left: Examples of marine mammals include:
● A male walrus *(Odobenus rosmarus)* with tusks, resting on an icy shelf;
● A harbor seal *(Phoca vitulina)* on an iceberg in Kenai Fjords National Park;
● A young polar bear *(Ursus maritimus)* staying close to its mother for protection; and
● Endangered Steller sea lions *(Eumetopias jubatus)* hauled out on a rocky shore.

◄ Near Dalton Highway, the snow-covered Brooks
Range is reflected in a lake following an August snowstorm.
▲ In early July, gull chicks step out on an iceberg
in Bear Glacier Lake near Seward.

◄ The North American porcupine
(Erethizon dorsatum) inhabits much of North America
from the Arctic Ocean to northern Mexico. The second-largest
rodent in North America, the porcupine is outsized only by the beaver.
▲ Devil's club *(Oplopanax horridus)* grows in trees in the rain forest of
Kupreanof Island, near Kake, in the Tongass National Forest. Both its
common name and its scientific name hint at its sharp spikes.

▲ The Hung Jury Ice Climb in Keystone
Canyon near Valdez offers mysterious-looking
frozen shapes formed by prevailing upstream winds.
▶ Bridal Veil Falls, in the Keystone Canyon, attracts ice
climbers from all over the country in January.

◄ St. Michael's, a Russian Orthodox Cathedral
originally built in 1848, is a major tourist attraction in Sitka.
▲ Aged by rain and covered with moss, grave markers at the Orthodox
Cemetery in Sitka show the distinctive shape of the Russian cross.
►► In Denali National Park, fall color is muted by clouds
hovering over the Thorofare Drainage.

▲ Hikers explore an ice canyon carved on
the surface of Matanuska Glacier, which is just a
two-hour drive from Anchorage along the Glenn Highway.
▶ A backpacker crosses the upper tributary of the Hulahula
River in the Arctic National Wildlife Refuge. The
Hulahula is also a favorite for rafters.

◄ Purple mountain saxifrage *(Saxifraga*
oppositifolia L ssp oppositifolia), surrounded by lichen, adorns
the Kongakut River Valley in the Alaska National Wildlife Refuge (ANWR).
▲ Newborn musk ox calves *(Ovibos moschatus)* investigate the world
near their mother on the North Slope of the Brooks Range.

▲ In 1896, North America's highest
mountain was officially named Mount McKinley, after U.S.
presidential candidate William McKinley. But in Alaska it has always been
known as Denali, which means "the great one" in the Dena'ina language.
Denali is the official name currently recognized by the State of Alaska.

▶ Horned puffin *(Fratercula corniculata)* are found along the
Pacific Coast from Oregon to Alaska and Siberia.

▲ The World's Largest Gold Nugget
"rests in peace" at the Gold Rush Cemetery in Skagway.
▶ Skagway's Town Harbor sports an interesting "flower garden":
empty purple bottles upended on "stems."

▲ Tlingit carver Nathan Jackson creates
his masterpieces at his studio in Saxman. His
work is coveted among collectors and museums.
► Playing at fish camp, a young girl from Hughes becomes
entangled as salmon dry on the spruce pole above her.

◄ Bunchberry *(Cornus canadensis)*
and wild rose *(Rosa acicularis)* decorate the
edges of Cottonwood Creek in the Matanuska Valley.
▲ Two pups of a rare silver subspecies of red fox *(Vulpes vulpes)*
play as they learn the skills they will need as adults.

▲ CLOCKWISE FROM TOP LEFT: Examples of Alaska's wildlife include:

◖ Mountain goats *(Oreamnos americanus)* with lambs on a snowfield;

◖ A black phase gray wolf *(Canis lupus)* on the coastal plain near the Jago River;

◖ Dall sheep *(Ovis dalli dalli)* in the deep December snow at Turnagain Arm; and

◖ Curious grizzly or brown bear cubs *(Ursus arctos horribilis)*, just 3 of
the more than 2,000 bears that roam Katmai National Park.

▲ In Denali National Park, the sod-roofed Kantishna
Mining District Recorders Office was built circa 1905.

▶▶ At about mile 120, the Parks Highway is adorned with a mix of
paper birch *(Betula papyrifera)*, which hybridizes with other birch trees;
fireweed *(Epilobium angustifolium)*, which can grow to nearly ten feet high; and
devil's club *(Echinopanax horridum)*, which causes dermatitis on contact.

▲ At Skagway, a steam locomotive awaits
passengers at the train yards for the White Pass and
Yukon Route Scenic Railroad. The narrow-gauge railroad was
built in 1898 during the Klondike gold rush. Billed as the
"Scenic Railway of the World," it is an International
Historic Civil Engineering Landmark.

▲ Broadway Street in Skagway presents a colorful,
quaint, but lazy face in the morning. Barroom pianos and
boomtown crowds still ring out in the night in Skagway,
famous as the historic gateway to the Klondike.

▲ A costumed Skagway Dolly Driver
washes the windows of her Yellow Tour Trolley.
▶ The McCabe Building, Alaska's first stone structure,
began as a boarding school for girls. Today, it serves as City
Hall and the Skagway Museum. City offices occupy
the second floor; museum exhibits, the first.

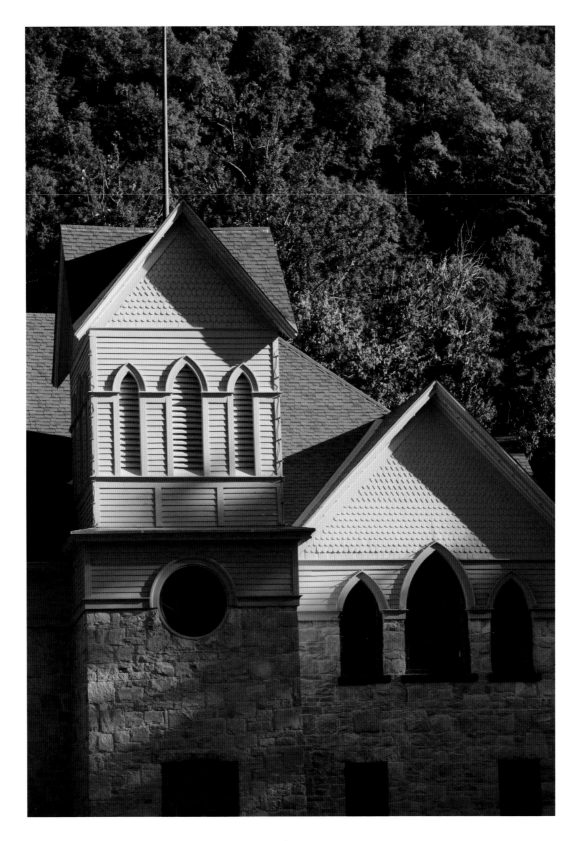

◄ Visitors check out the observation
deck at a Mount Roberts Tram Station.
Construction on the tram was completed in 1997.
▲ The tram takes visitors 1,800 feet above Juneau, affording
stunning views of the town and harbor. At the top, attractions
include a restaurant, a theater, and Native artworks,
as well as an extensive trail system.

107

▲ One of the most enjoyable
benefits of hiking and river rafting in the
backcountry is camping out in beautiful places.
Here, the campsite is set up alongside the Copper River.
► In early July, a backpacker camps on a ridge above the Hulahula
River in the Arctic National Wildlife Refuge.

▲ A ten-day celebration of Alaska's fur
trapping and trading heritage, the Fur Rendezvous
includes a fireworks display over the Anchorage skyline.
▶ In Alaska, Nature puts on a fireworks display of its own: the
aurora is visible from the Interior an average of 240 nights a year.
▶▶ Just follow the signs and you won't get lost. A directional sign in Homer
seems to point the way to everywhere in Alaska—all at once.